Alternative Thinking

Moshe Wilker, M.D.

ISBN (Print Edition): 978-1-54396-954-2

ISBN (eBook Edition): 978-1-54396-955-9

ALTERNATIVE THINKING

MOSHE WILKER, M.D.

1

Experience with the non-self

Although you may find this book on a shelf of a self-improvement section, it is not meant for that. It is a guide to the truth of what exists. The truth is that what you think is not fully true. This includes who you think you are.

The ideas presented in this book will most likely not be believable or acceptable as the brain always rejects not using itself. Without transcendental meditation these ideas are just another leap of faith. You are not being asked to make that leap. You are not being asked to believe what I say or my experiences. After you meditate you should conclude these ideas on your own. Only through experience of non-self, these ideas will become acceptable. Your non-self is your first person without any identification, thought, or characteristic.

2

Perfection is inefficient

Perfection is a good example of the emotional ambiguity of language. Perfection is supposed to be something good. It is supposed to be something we strive for. The truth is that striving for perfection at many times means we are dissatisfied. Trying to achieve perfection means you are not content with the now.

It takes a smaller amount of your time to perform most of the job.

It takes an additional larger amount of your time to perfect your job.

That time, energy and awareness used in your efforts could be used for other tasks.

Emotions are the physiological manifestation of feelings

In life, emotions and feelings are used interchangeably but I like to differentiate them for the sake of communication. Feelings are subconscious interpretations (ie thoughts) whereas emotions are physical. Here are some examples:

Crying is the physiological manifestation of feeling sadness (the interpretation that you are not going to get what you want)

Smiling is the physiological manifestation of feeling of happiness (the interpretation that you are going to get what you want)

Heart racing is the physiological manifestation of feeling scared (the interpretation that you are in danger)

4

You are reflexes of association.

No one truly knows where our feelings come from. Some may say it comes from our soul but in my opinion the most logical explanation is that they are shortcuts for the algorithm of thinking we have developed from previous experiences.

Therefore, I would argue that feelings can also be known as beliefs, subconscious and thoughts.

The subconscious is not a big unknown (as the famous picture of only the tip of the iceberg is visible above water) but rather a shortcut of association from previous experiences where the actual experience has been forgotten. You cannot unlearn a reflex but if you are aware of the universe rather than your thoughts you can learn an alternative reflex.

The past situations may have been rationale, but their shortcuts are no longer rational and therefore may be inappropriate. If these are the basis of our thoughts, then the thoughts they produce have an irrational basis.

Familiar environment will trigger these feelings. The evolutionary purpose of these feelings is to efficiently interpret the environment as positive or negative.

(5)

Do not believe your beliefs.

If you can do this then you are enlightened because you become aware to what is.

This state increases acceptance of the universe since you are not listening to your "self" you are a part of everything.

If you eliminate your thoughts, you eliminate yourself and whats the left is the truth of existence.

6

You are not a singular soul but many independent thoughts.

This explains the pathology of split personality or hearing voices.

The Soul is used interchangeably by society with gut feeling, spirit, voice in head, god and devil, energy, subconscious, identity, personality, and ego among others.

The subconscious reflexes of feelings are not a single entity but a compilation of many independent goals.

That is why a suicidal man may say that he cannot live with himself.

If your soul is based on your past, and your past no longer exist but a copy in your head then your soul is based on that copy. Since there are many pasts there are many copies and many souls.

This explains why you may contradict yourself at different times. This also explains the argument you may have with yourself when undecisive.

7

Free will is an oxymoron

Since you are reflexes of interpretations that trigger your thoughts you don't have free will.

As a matter of fact, your will is confining you to follow specific learned patterns. What happens when your wills conflict one another?

For instance, at one time you may crave something sweet because you interpreted that it will give you pleasure but at another time you may not want to have something sweet because you interpreted that you will gain unnecessary weight.

We are not in control

Thoughts are not produced by you because at times you do not agree with them, they constantly change, and they make you lose control leading to regret. Our thoughts are controlling us.

9

There is no goal or purpose to your life

Since your wills, goals and purpose is to follow your beliefs which are not of one you then there is no need or want to do anything.

10

Accept the unknown

The mechanism of action of meditation is a mystery but that is the whole point. It is about accepting the unknown. You are preforming an act that is against your nature, to disregard your own thought. This eventually eliminates yourself so that for the rest of the day you can create alternate experiences.

Removing your thoughts (shutting down firing neurons) allows for increased awareness of the now because interpretations based on your past are not actually here.

Unknown is the opposite of interpretation.

(11)

Thinking uses up awareness.

Awareness is your brains potential energy whereas thinking is your brains kinetic energy. It is also known as attention or experience.

Awareness has the capacity to think. More thoughts occupying awareness means less awareness of each. This means that each thought will rely more on subconscious using old patterns of association. In the selfless state, such as after meditation where thoughts are ignored, one can think more clearly as there is less to juggle.

12

To be or to think, that is the question

Your awareness also known as consciousness, being, presence, experience, and observer.

Your awareness is not you, it is yours. "you" implies you are a separate entity from anything that is not "you".

Your awareness is your potential energy to observe.

Without thoughts our awareness becomes available to our senses. We are satisfied with what is because we don't interpret anything as good versus bad. we do not get distracted by feelings, so we are more focus on the task at hand. We are free to alternatives.

When we do have a single thought, it has room to expand and become more comprehensive.

Without thinking it is easier to say So what and have all the time in the world.

Subconscious thoughts are separate independent learned reflexes that are designed by evolution to pursue survival. This is no less than an uncontrolled cancerous cell.

If try to pay attention to multiple things at same time, then will resort to patterns because it is more efficient.

The more thoughts you have the less you are aware of each and therefore rely on subconscious reflexes. The less thoughts you have the more you are aware of each and rely less on subconscious reflexes. This allows to revise subconscious reflexes as you gain new perspective thru experience of an alternate response to stimuli.

13

Minimize your thinking

Thoughts and awareness are inversely correlated. The more thoughts, the less awareness you have and vice versa.

We can never completely stop thinking as thinking is a reflex. But what we can do is minimize our thoughts through transcendental meditation. Thinking is brain activity. You cannot use brain activity to stop thinking.

Transcendental meditation focuses on only one brain activity (the mantra) and trains to disassociate awareness of any other thought. This cleans your mind from everything but the mantra. After about 30 minutes there will be less thoughts to dissociate from so the session is completed. The session may or may not be difficult as your thoughts may resist being ignored but with practice eventually, they will be ignored. After a successful session when thoughts have been removed, new thoughts from subconscious reflexes will be easier to disassociate because of your increased capacity of awareness. Following a successful session of meditation until you go to sleep where subconscious thrives you would experience a truthful experience of life. Disassociating from thoughts allow for being in the moment, letting go, mindfulness, bliss, peace, ambiguity of truth, learning, alternatives, creativity, and freedom from orders ("will") from "self".

In transcendental meditation you give up yourself.

14

Our thoughts are the foundation
of our realities.

One cannot think that a reality does not exist because reality is based on thinking. If reality does not exist then our thoughts are wrong, and if our thoughts are wrong then how can you think that reality does not exist. Therefore, the only way to prove that reality does not exist is to not think. When you do not think only what exists remains. By experiencing this existence, you can repair false realities.

15

The truth is ambiguous

The delusion of your reality is preventing your awareness to other alternatives of the truth.

There are infinite correct but different realities (interpretations of what exist) depending on subjective perspective.

The Truth is also known as existence and "the here and now". It is objective. It can be sensed with your five senses.

Reality, on the other hand, is an illusionary, single perspective, and subjective interpretation of the truth. It is created by your brain using the past and future. Everyone's reality is slightly different than each other.

16

You are the creator of your reality which you then become aware of.

Reality is the product of thought in your brain using reflexes from past to make decisions regarding your future. You feel this reality rather than sense it. your reflexes are by nature chasing comforts. You must obey them otherwise you will "feel" uncomfortable.

Your reality is not the same someone else although it may be similar in what exists. This is just like one copier machine will never look the same as another copier machine of the same document.

Your subconscious reflexes are meant to achieve pleasure and avoid suffering. This is an impossible pursuit as the universe is constantly changing. Such reflexes, if go unchecked, compile a reality of good and bad feelings.

(17)

Do not pursue happiness as it
is relative not absolute.

Happiness is when you think you achieved what you wanted. It is not sustainable and if we keep trying to pursue it, we would only be disappointed. Without thoughts there is no positive vs negative or happiness vs sadness. There is only satisfaction and acceptance since everything including your awareness is connected.

Without using subconscious thoughts comparing to past or future, happiness or sadness do not exist. Therefore, happiness is contingent on also experiencing its opposite, sadness.

(18)

If Thoughts are an illusion in the brain,
then the thinker as well as the reality
it produces are illusions as well.

Thoughts are interpretation of what exist. this interpretation though is a copy of what exists. A copy is not the original and therefore can have mistaken.

If thoughts are a copy or illusion, then the thinker as well as the reality it produces is an illusion.

If the thinker and the reality is just an illusionary interpretation, then it can have mistaken.

Such common mistakes include the illusion of separatism of self and the illusion of the need to improve self.

19

Thoughts cause separatism.

Since you are the subject of thinking then everything else is the object.

By thinking you are creating a separation between you, the thinker, and everything that you are thinking about. This creates an illusion of separatism. If you are not one but many neuronal reflexes, then this separatism does not exist.

Without identifying with your thoughts you are in harmony with the world

$$(20)$$

Thoughts, led by the illusion of self,
are mostly concerned with improving
comfort of future self, based on
the self's past experiences.

They try to improve comfort or avoid pain based on previous experiences. Depending on the thought of successfulness then happiness or sadness may ensue.

21

Be selfless

Not selfless in sense of generosity because generosity still originates in a self-agenda. It also doesn't mean to do what others want. It only means to be able to shut down your thoughts so that you can be aware of what exist around you.

(22)

You cannot learn something new when
you think you already know it.

By removing most of your thoughts in meditation, you are allowing to remove yourself (since you are the source of your thoughts). This is how you change your belief system.

you must first remove your belief in order to allow for a new experience of an alternate belief.

After meditation is the time where access to alternate beliefs can turn into a new reality. After experiencing environment naturally, we create another believable reality again that cannot be changed.

By letting go of thinking you let go of the automatic self serving distortion of existence which appears as reality. Only the truth of existence remains to be awared of.

(23)

Intention and guided meditation, although may be relaxing, do not shut down your interpretations and therefore will not allow to reach state of selflessness.

Because guidance and intention require thinking, they do not get rid of self during the session.

During the session you may feel relaxed because you are distracting yourself from negative thinking but after the session your brain will find something to worry about.

To optimize your meditation, you need to remove external stimulation that may trigger your brain to interpret.

(24)

Meditation has short term and long-term effects

The short-term effect last for the rest of your day after meditation in which you already detached from most of your subconscious thoughts. You therefore become more aware of what is for the rest of the day. This increased awareness will expose you to alternatives, but it disappears after you go to sleep. This increased awareness will not impact your personality by itself.

The long-term effect happens naturally when you develop new alternative thinking from your daily increased awareness. This will impact your personality.

25

Dreaming is subconscious
and unchecked thinking

It is a chain of thoughts based on pf and completely disconnected from the now. it can happen when awake or sleep.

The problem with multiple thoughts is that you get lost in them. They create a reality manifested by your brain. An interpreted reality triggers a thought that creates a reality that triggers a thought, etc.

Human beings have the best evolutionary design to automatically create thoughts. The problem arises that we do not automatically stop them. Meditation allows you to refocus away from your thoughts.

Placebo is a false interpretation

An accurate scientific experiment will prevent a placebo effect. Placebo is the manifestation of thought into reality. This means that the placebo does not exist. it is an illusion.

(27)

Genuine love is selfless.

Love is when something or someone makes you think that you are more comfortable with it than without it. Genuine love, however, has nothing to do with you.

$$\left(\ 28\ \right)$$

Care is a selfish concern

When you love you care. You are concerned with making sure that it stays by you because it makes you comfortable.

Genuine love though actually has no care because you know that you are many neurons rather than one entity and therefore although some of your neurons may enjoy it, you do not need it by you.

(29) Knowledge is prison

You may hear knowledge is power but this power just like everything else has its downside. The downside is that it prevents you from seeing any alternative knowledge and therefore inhibits your awareness of the truth which is ambiguous. Your knowledge prevents you from free awareness which prevents free thinking.

(30)

Changing beliefs require not just understanding but also removal.

You may notice that sometimes you understand the rationale of a reality, but you cannot actually do it. this is because you have developed the neurons for this pattern but there are other conflicting neurons that are preventing its execution.

Therefore, you must also remove or disbelieve any conflicting thoughts.

(31)

Killing your self

That is what is being practiced at meditation. You are ignoring yourself. This removes your reality and reality includes the interpretation of self. You become familiar with a disownment of self.

32

You are the creator of the
reality that controls you

Your brain produces a reality which you then become aware of and you then you respond to it with more thinking.

This cycle is self perpetuating.

33

I think therefore I was

The famous I think therefore I am should really be changed to past tense. This is because every thought you have was generated seconds ago and therefor belongs to the past and does not exist. in the present you are aware of it.

(34)

You are both the generator and the receiver.

The generator is your brain producing thoughts. Your brain is a system of beliefs created by previous experiences.

The receiver is your awareness of those thoughts. You do not have to believe them.

The generator and receiver are mutually exclusive. The more you believe the less you are aware and vice versa.

(35)

Habits are the manifestations of thinking patterns

You may have habits which don't make sense to you or you may not agree with at certain time and place. The reason you don't understand why you have these habits is because they are result of a learned thinking pattern. perhaps this habit used to provide you pleasure and now its already programmed as a reflex. The only way to remove such habits is to stop thinking.

(36)

To be enlighten is to accept not knowing.

When you know then you are not open to alternatives. When you do not know, or at least not certain, then you may access alternative knowledge and create alternative patterns

(37)

Self awareness is not important.

Not only its not important, it is the problem. To become aware of yourself is to become aware of multiple illusions, some of which conflict each other. It is much truer to have nonself awareness as you become aware to what exist without the filter of self.

(38)

Nothing requires your concern.

The universe will go on with or without you. Since reality is your illusions, nothing in it really matters as much as you think it does. All your goals and sense of purpose is illusionary. You do not need to alter or fix anything as everything is already working in a dynamic equilibrium as a whole.

(39)

Reality appears true when
you cannot unthink it.

Since we do not naturally unthink, reality appears real. It appears as if it's the original existing form. If we were able to naturally unthink then reality would be constantly changing. This would be truer, but the thinker would find it vulnerable. The discomfort of vulnerability is preventing us from experience the truth.

(40)

In order to change beliefs, you must change how you view reality

Your beliefs become your reality. If you wanted to change just one belief, i.e. the fear of flying, it would be difficult since you cannot just change one thing that appears as real. Every time you will go on airplane you will have the fear which will only reinforce the reality. The better way is to change how you view your entire reality. By accepting dismissal of reality as an illusion of the truth you can see what exists during flight. After a few such flights that will go without fear your belief would change.

(41)

Boredom is the minds activity not inactivity

You are bored when you are dissatisfied with the lack of value of the current status quo. Such interpretation triggers mind to think of ways to change the present situation. When your mind is stopped and is at rest you will become more aware and appreciate the present situation without the discomfort of its seemingly lack of value.

(42)

your consciousness cannot be hurt

Hurting is an interpretation of thought. You can sense the potentially painful stimulus, but it will not hurt unless you interpret it as pain.

(43)

The means justify the end

Since you are always in the now, the means are more important than the end goal. The means exist while the end is an illusion.

44

We are defined not by an inherent soul but by how we have programmed to interact with the world.

We always think in the now but because time and space keep changing so do your thoughts. At any space and time, you have a thought that came from you now but at another space and time a conflicting thought may appear like its coming from you now as well. This is how we are connected to the world.

(45)

Knowledge is the cause for suffering

Without knowledge there would not be opposites. There wouldn't be happiness or sadness. There wouldn't be good or bad. There would not be ugly or beautiful. Without opposites there would not be a need to chase the better one because everything is neutral.

(46)

The god people believe in
is your subconscious

Your subconscious is the creator of reality

Your subconscious determines good vs bad

Your subconscious works in mysterious ways because you do not remember the experiences that caused your patterns.

Voices of god are voices of your subconscious

(47)

We are addicted to everything

When speaking of addiction, people usually refer to a pathological addiction such as smoking and overeating which have deleterious health effects. But when speaking of addiction as something that you cannot live without could refer to sitting a certain way, eating a certain food, having a certain hobby, talking with a certain volume, holding the wheel in a certain way. Most of the things we do without putting attention into them are occurring in an automatic way that just feels more comfortable.

48

Ignoring thought frees your mind

When you are unable to ignore a thought, you identify with it as coming from yourself. This creates a rigid perspective and hinders creativity. Its harder to ignore a fully developed thought because it becomes a reality but if you can ignore it before getting lost in it you will maintain your presence in the now and continue to witness what exists. If you have a commentator that you could not ignore, then it would be perceived as you since its always there and no one else can hear it. If you could truly ignore that commentator before it even makes a comment, then you will realize that the commentator is not you.

(49)

Our reality is biased by self-preservation

As our thoughts create our reality, they are designed by evolution to survive and reproduce. This alters the truth and attracts us to solve problems that are not even there.

50

A false is mistakenly believable
when it is surrounded by trues

Some may take advantage of this when want to lie to someone for personal gain. For the most part though this is an innocent error. When getting information from a source that you know for the most part is correct one can easily believe a false new information as true because most other information was true based on personal experience. The more information is true, the more believable the false new information will be. This is the double edge sword of a reliable source.

(51)

Your brain is the most reliable
source but that is the problem.

When your brain is misinterpreting you will not be able to notice its falsehood when you are depending on your brain to interact with environment. Since for the most part our brain serves us well, we continue listening to its advice without question.

(52)

Comforts will not make you comfortable permanently

When you act to comfort a discomfort, you may be successful but only temporarily. This problem leads to patterns and possibly a pathological addiction. The best solution is accepting your discomfort until it becomes comfortable. A discomfort is a dissatisfaction with the now. If you believe this interpretation you will try to amend it. The problem is that you will continue trying to amend it forever until you stop believing yourself.

(53)

Existence plus thought equals reality

Existence is also known as the truth, now, experience, presence and being.

Thought is also known as belief and feelings. It comes from past experiences through learning.

Because everyone's previous experiences are different so is everyone's reality. the only way to experience existence instead of reality is in meditation because that is the only place that thoughts can be removed. The experience of existence allows you to learn to be comfortable with not using thoughts.

54

We cannot stop thinking but we
can stop listening to thoughts.

Since thinking is a reflex to a trigger, one cannot stop thinking. Once a thought is triggered though we can stop listening to it. This is usually uncomfortable because your brain feels that your wellbeing depends on completing the thought. With meditation you can get comfortable with it.

(55)

Since thinking is a verb, theres
a subject and an object.

The subject is the thinker, the object is the reality. Every thought thinks it comes from the same origin of a constant self. It is therefore uncomfortable not to listen to yourself. Ignoring yourself may appear as if you are turning yourself off and you will cease to exist. In transcendental meditation, without thinking the "I" is removed and so does the reality it produces. You experience your continued existence with not having to listen to yourself. This experience makes it more comfortable to do so outside of meditation.

(56)

Thinking triggers thinking

Once a thought is completed it produces a reality which can just as well trigger another thought process. This is self-perpetuating. If one is comfortable with disassociating from a thought, then this vicious cycle can be stopped.

(57)

Attention without speculation

Our subjective reality already provides us with preset interpretations. Such reality obstructs our attention. Without speculation we can pay more attention to what exists and therefore be more in harmony with the truth.

Your gut is full of crap

Many advise to listen to your gut. The actual gut cannot give advice. It is your brain's subconscious thought that triggers an autonomic response in your body. your nervous system is set up to prepare body to whats happening in environment. The heart may need to beat faster during a fight or flight response. It may feel like your body is interpreting the environment, but it is your body reacting to your brain's interpretation of the environment. If your subconscious thought is erroneous or inappropriate, then even though your body may "feel" a certain way does not mean you should pay attention to it.

(59)

We think therefore we are

I think therefore I am makes sense for a single thought, but we have multiple thoughts at same time. These thoughts may contradict each other. Eventually you pick one thought to represent you best but the thought that is picked can be different at different times. This means that a single thought is not necessarily a true representation of who you are. In fact, the multiple thoughts you have are a better representation of who you are. This means that there are many of you.

60

When you can let go of a thought
you can disown yourself

Disowning yourself or losing your identity does not seem like a good thing at first. If, however, there is no one self then you are only disowning what appears as yourself but is not. This is useful because it allows to resolve conflict within yourselves. It allows you to adapt to the changing environment. it makes room for creative ideas.

61

When a thought is not completed then
it lingers and occupies attention

A thought can be completed either by execution of the thought or by dismissing it. executing all your thoughts will turn out to be contradictory to each other. Dismissing thoughts therefore is important to know. Transcendental meditation allows for one to practice how to do it.

62

Agree to disagree

Just because someone disagrees with you, does not make either of you is selfish or stubborn. Selfishness is when you cannot agree to disagree because you think you are the center of the universe and only your reality is correct. You are each following your own reality which is based on your personal past. Stubbornness is when you resist someone or something. When agreeing to disagree you are not resisting but accepting someone or something as different.

(63)

Your reality is what your thoughts say it is.

Your thoughts interpret your reality. Only experience can revise your thoughts. By experiencing how to dismiss thoughts you can change your reality. Changing your reality will allow new experiences which will revise your thoughts.

64

Say no to yourself

When there is a problem in life it is not in the apparent subject of the thought which appears to be the environment but the inception of the thought in the first place. It seems easy to get rid of our problems by just not listening to our thoughts but when many thoughts are already firing, this is difficult because we identify with them. We think that without our thought something bad will happen.

65

You are more than yourself

Your self is a robot that produces automatic interpretation of reality in order to survive. Although this robot is a part of you, you are more than just your robot. You are your attention. You cannot shut the robot completely, but you can turn it down.

(66)

The more you expose yourself to
discomfort the lower the threshold
would be for comfort.

This can also be said vice versa. The more you resist discomfort the higher the threshold would be to get comfort.

67

Meditation trains you to let go.

Meditation is a workout; it is not the same as passive relaxation. When you listen to music or watch a beautiful view, you are not meditating (at least not in the definition that is described in this book), you are passively relaxing by attending something pleasant. Although this is calming and peaceful, it will not prevent a stress when these pleasant things are not there.

In meditation you exercise ignoring any thought that goes in your brain thereby preventing it from perpetuating.

(68)

A mind occupied by thought is
analogous to a sink full of water.

The sink itself represents the mind. The water in it represents your thoughts. When your mind is fully occupied by thoughts then theres no room for any additional thoughts especially those that are required right now.

When we meditate, we are opening the drain.

(69)

There are short- and long-term effects of meditation

The short-term effect is that your mind emptied of thoughts has a capacity to accept new thoughts. This is "clearing your mind". This can also occur whenever focusing your attention on something else such as a game or a task. This is analogous to the sink opening the drain but closing it right after the activity ends. Everyone's sink is different. Mine usually fills up again within a day.

The long-term effect is what makes meditation special. The practice of meditation trains you to open the drain voluntarily at any time not dependent on distracting with another activity.

Feelings vs. senses

Feelings are subjective interpretations of your brain. They are based on your past and are imaginary in their source. Feelings create an altered reality in which time does not exist. They can be created out of thought or even a sense. For example, the suffering aspect of pain is the feeling of the sense of nociception).

Senses are objective and only occur in the now. There are many of them such as taste, smell, touch, nociception, balance, etc. Their purpose of these senses though evolution is to interact the body with the environment it is in.

Senses are the only way to detect the truth of the here and now. all the feelings that arise from these senses have already been interpreted subjectively.

71

Feelings are concepts of your
subjective imagination.

Feelings such as worry, fear, comfort and boredom are only true as your reality. there's nothing wrong with having these feelings but one should know that they can be turned off by letting go of the thoughts that produced the reality.